RED RADIO HEART

✻ ✻ ✻

OTHER BOOKS OF POETRY BY JANE LUNIN PEREL

The Lone Ranger and the Neo-American Church
Archival Press, 1975

The Fishes
Providence College Press, 1977

Blowing Kisses to the Sharks
Copper Beech Press, 1978

The Sea Is Not Full
Le'dory Publishing House, Tel Aviv, 1990

RED RADIO HEART

Prose Poems

* * *

Jane Lunin Perel

For Marisa,
I admire your
energy!! You
Thrive!! fondly,
Jane 11/5/12

WHITE PINE PRESS / BUFFALO, NEW YORK

WHITE PINE PRESS
P.O. BOX 236
BUFFALO, NEW YORK 14201
www.whitepine.org

ACKNOWLEDGMENTS

Many thanks to the editors of the following publications where these poems
first appeared, sometimes in a slightly different form: "Blood Somewhere," *The
Prose Poem: An International Journal; The Best of the Prose Poem: An International Journal*.
"Pleading Insanity," *The Prose Poem: An International Journal; Sentence*. "Isis," *Sentence*.
"Art History," "Buna," "Commuter Train," "Fall of Leningrad," "Lamb's Head,"
"Louie Loves Kids," "Pastrami," "Wedding," "Insomniac's List," "Mermaid," *The
Alembic*. "Greens," under the title "Portion Control," *Flights*. "Hospice,"
TygerBurning.

My thanks go to Providence College for its continued support of my work and
the recent sabbatical during which I wrote many of these poems and completed
this manuscript. I thank all the students I have been fortunate enough to study
with and who have inspired me. Also I wish to thank the MacDowell Colony for
the residency out of which many of these poems were born.

I have always appreciated my daughter Marissa's faith in my work.

My sister Andrea's support is invaluable.

Thanks to Eve Broffman for her technical support.

Cover design: Keith Marques

First Edition.

ISBN: 978-1-935210-34-4

Printed and bound in the United States of America.

Library of Congress Control Number: 2012931167

Contents

Part Two

Introduction

✻ ✻ ✻

What makes someone who has been writing verse poetry for forty years suddenly write a book of prose poems? Boredom? Or is some higher, unconscious imperative at work? In a way, it doesn't matter as long as the book is worth reading, and, in Jane Lunin Perel's case, *Red Radio Heart* passes the test, adding to a small list of unique collections of prose poems written over the last ten years. The book also enlarges on a subgenre of the prose poem: the sequence revolving around certain themes, one or more characters, or both.

Perel has always been a champion of confessional poetry, and many of her verse poems echo the imagery and intensity of Plath's. They can be painful, but, unlike Plath, Perel is often celebratory. One of my favorite poems is called "The Bath," written on her daughter's first birthday. It is a poem rooted in realistic imagery, and yet the rhythm and line breaks, the constant ruminating on the cleansing ritual, approach incantation. "There is nothing on earth but the rain- / bow in the splashing and the oriental / chimes of the water and our fingers lace / as we hum, as I rock on my knees over you and / we make our duet of water and air." The poem ends with the narrator "bent, tired, and wet," "though somehow never / younger or stronger," as her daughter utters in their "sweet / rolling bath for the first time Mama."

So much confessional poetry fails because the poet wallows in despair, or conversely, sees every trivial personal experience as being noteworthy.   So much of it encourages verbal self-indulgence. But Perel has always been a master at being both expressive and disciplined, at effortlessly juxtaposing, sometimes in the same poem, the tragic and the joyful.

We see many of the above strengths in *Red Radio Heart*, but whereas in Perel's verse poetry she corrals and shapes emotion through careful use of line breaks, in *Red Radio Heart*, she cuts loose. I am reminded of Baudelaire's dream of a poetic prose "supple and rugged enough to adapt itself to the lyrical impulses of the soul, the undulations of reverie, the jibes of conscience." What a perfect description of *Red Radio Heart*.

Red Radio Heart chronicles the trials and tribulations of a character named Carnelia. The poems explore her relationship with her husband and daughter, with her sisters, and with her father. But it is also a book about being a woman, particularly about being a Jewish woman and a feminist. Old myths make appearances too, as do many absurd not-so-newsworthy events that continually pummel Carnelia as she tries to get on with life. A young poet fresh from an MFA program couldn't have written this collection. First, she wouldn't have lived long enough to possess Perel's experiences and knowledge; secondly, she wouldn't have had the patience or wisdom to shape those experiences into poetry, to overhear the poems speaking with each other.

But the prose poem also accounts for some of the success of *Red Radio Heart.* Whether Perel consciously chose the form or the form chose her, the prose poem, by its very nature, allows her to roam freely between different time periods, moods, and verbal registers. That is, to steal Bly's terminology, the prose poem gives her permission to "leap" toward, instead of away from, the unconscious.

And, boy, does she leap.

Consider the title poem of the collection, "Red Radio Heart."
Carnelia is tired of her heart. It's too heavy. When
she tries to sleep it bumps, then races. She pictures it,
disentangling itself from the system that feeds it, then
shrinking, escaping out of her mouth, rolling down the
street. Sticky candy apple heart. Road kill heart. She
could have a pig's heart. Or a red radio heart that would
play jazz for her but not Bartok. Her heart in a yellow
basket that Ella Fitzgerald has lost. Maybe Frankenstein
will stagger out from behind the billboard that supports
the war. He'll need a new heart, too. Maybe he'll scoop
up hers and she'll be free of her clumsy overripe blood
orange heart. Meanwhile, the generals beef up attacks.

What amazing shifts in this poem! Think of how simply we begin
in the first line with the poet's matter-of-fact use of an old
metaphor. Then the leaping starts, the metaphors becoming wilder,
the free play of imagination broken temporarily by fragments, so we
can shift from Carnelia's heart to one of a pig, to one of a radio that
is playing jazz, which throughout the book often signals, like a good
expressionistic play, her father's presence. Then Frankenstein (a guy
with an estranged heart) emerges, the poem ending, ironically, with
heartless generals beefing up attacks. So much happening in such a
short space, yet the images aren't arbitrary. Throughout *Red Radio
Heart*, Perel becomes the lightning rod for seemingly incompatible
experiences, and her maturity keeps all these forces from drifting
into incoherency.

But be forewarned, reader, *Red Radio Heart* is not, if you'll excuse
the play on words, for the faint of heart. One poem opens,
"Carnelia is walking for herself and for those who cannot walk—
the dead, whose legs of dust support her, and the living, lying in
gauze, watching their own embalming." There are poems, too,
about the indignities of fighting cancer and trips to concentration
camps. But there is also an odd sense of humor pervading the

book, one that comes from begrudgingly accepting the crap life throws us. Also, how can a book that so often celebrates nature's eternal presence not be uplifting? How can we not be drawn to a voice that embraces a very powerful feminine life force, as described so beautifully in "dew."

> Voices come to Carnelia as she wakes . . . dew whispers, "I depose the roses' sleep with dawn's blood. My wet jag daggering tight blooms. You can wash your feet, in my cool pearls, prepare yourself for the fires of noon." How can Carnelia explain to anyone that this is her religion?

Perhaps Carnelia isn't up to the task, but Perel accomplishes it expertly throughout *Red Radio Heart.*

—Peter Johnson

PART ONE

✳ ✳ ✳

…"sitting on a trick coffin in a cream-colored straight jacket, he's fed chunks of sirloin by the Bird Girl. "My whole life," he says, "I've been chasing the sound of my mother's heartbeat." Inside the ebony box a woman is weeping."

From "Houdini"
by Peter Johnson

Blowtorch

The Moon is Carnelia's locksmith. She shall not be locked. The Moon leadeth her through the roaring galaxy, lasers her in the path of left handedness for Her name's sake. Yea, though Carnelia bounds through the cosmos, the Moon calls her back. Carnelia shall fear no image, no knowledge, for Thou art with her. Thy blowtorch centers her. Thou preparest a table for her in the presence of all humanity. Thou unlocks her psyche with juniper oil. Carnelia's soul runneth over. Surely orchid throats will follow Carnelia all the days of her life. She will dwell in the tent of the Moon. Forever.

Mermaid

Carnelia is watching the premier of "Mermaid Girl" at 9:00, perhaps
"Paralyzed and Pregnant" at 10:00. Shiloh the mermaid girl is the
only living mermaid. Sirenomelia is the term: one fused leg, a foot
twisted inside, one ovary, no large intestine, no rectum, no vagina,
half a kidney. She's had forty surgeries in her seven years. Her
mom says, "No one has told her she's supposed to die." Shiloh
loves butterflies, purple and pink. She says "Some people like me
the way I am." She laughs and a million balloons burst. She paints
her fingernails magenta, squirts the doctor with a hypodermic
before he draws her blood. She adores her parents and they all get
by with jokes.

The fat child in Carnelia who did not meet her mother's standards
loves Shiloh, wants to play with her. For a moment Carnelia thinks
she is Shiloh, unable to walk or balance but ripe with games, always
different, always the other. But no, Carnelia is a two legged woman.
A klutz in ballet, the tutu so tight over her shaking belly the
audience laughed at her. What was she doing on the stage with all
those skinny Irish girls? Her mother was humiliated, but Shiloh's
mother is beyond shame. Her love is thick pink, like taffy.
Carnelia's shuts off the T.V. and dreams Shiloh is waiting for her to
ride the seesaw, to hold her hand. Carnelia finds her in the seaside
cottage her parents rented in Maine. They swim together, flying
over waves. In the morning Shiloh is with her, helping her to walk.
Thank you Shiloh, Carnelia whispers.

The universe spins on Shiloh's laughter and The Maker shrugs.

Blood Somewhere

Carnelia does not know what to think of the world-renowned Doctor on whose walls glide eight striped wooden fish with aluminum eyes, cork pupils. Fish with chrome tails swimming like zombies, whistling voodoo tunes. They are next to the eight black and white prints of rotting cauliflower across from the mandala of hemp and dried blood. "Did you have the blood? Somewhere else?" the receptionist asks over the phone. Did someone lose her blood? Carnelia wonders. Or store it in an unsafe place, a refrigerator in a slum that Dobermans snarl at? The door to the office is solid mahogany, framed in black. The handle is chrome that shines like a scalpel. It's supposed to calm you, these off-white walls and recessed lighting, black leather seating. But Carnelia thinks if she stands up and walks to the door, opening it, a zebra will romp in with a red mouth and a gash under its left eye. It will track her until she rushes into the Doctor's private office where she will find him X-raying fish, his hands raw from washing.

Art History

By 1926 Lorca was passionate over Dali. He hated women's breasts but Dali painted them in pairs, flying. Carnelia's eyes widen while reading the art history article. She goes downstairs to make lemonade. She bows her head over the lemons and powdered sugar. She's making it for the Tai Kwando Master's son, who'll soon be arriving, like a whirlwind, taking each room apart, then skipping to the next. He likes to say words over and over. "Lemons. Lemons. Lemons." His hair is raven black, like Dali's. Carnelia can picture him at twenty-two with Dali's mustache, Lorca chasing him behind the grape arbor. She will finish the reading when it's cooler. Meanwhile she grips each lemon and squeezes until her palm burns. She feels a green tongue licking her calf. Her dog Chow Mein clambers for water.

Commuter Train

Amber puts blush on in the car. "Make-up takes you from corpse to queen." Nine months after careening into a tree while tubing down a slope, she's taking a commuter train to Boston. Carnelia watches Amber hobble with her decoupaged cane to the platform's outdoor bench. It's cold and no one but Amber waits. She's going to hear her friend Julie sing at a bar. A man comes along. Carnelia can see them talking. "One sudden move, I'll deck you," Carnelia warns through the windshield. She can see herself leaping over the track from the parking lot. She has to pee so badly she's cross-eyed, but she will not leave until Amber is on the train. The man keeps his distance. They enter the car and the train throttles past, Amber disappearing. Carnelia cries, which doesn't help her bladder. What guts Amber has, titanium hip, titanium elbow, pain killers in her bag. A fawn limping to water, her fire-red hair perfect under any neon light. A shooting star of a woman, part of her frozen, part of her on fire, ready for the city to take her in and the sculptor she'll meet.

Double Scythe

Amber formed in Carnelia—the dark side of the moon pressing against the double scythe of the May moon, full flower moon, full corn planting moon, full milk moon.* That is why the moon is their tent, their shared light, then and now, the black birth onyx soldered to the opal of the bitten fruit. The moon fixes her veiled eye that lacks a pupil over Amber and Carnelia, dissolving the distance between them. Amber finger-paints. Shooting stars go off behind Carnelia's eyes.

*"May Moon to Full Milk Moon,"
"The Natural World: Full Moon Names and Dates,"
Farmer's Almanac, 2007.

Closing Bone

Carnelia learns to meditate. She's at the train station again, floating toward the domed ceiling. She is chocolate melting, fire rising. Each chakra opening after so long. Tonight she'll dream of the paralyzed actor rising out of his wheel chair like a swan in snow. Now Amber walks forward on her cane, her perfect small body twisted from the accident and titanium rods. After nine months, she has visited Joachim in Brooklyn and watched dancers leap to his electronic music. Then he carried her up the six flights to his loft. Now she is back with Ari and Carnelia until spring when the earth will break open. Until then Carnelia will take her to the acupuncturist, the internist, the post traumatic stress expert, the chiropractor, the orthopedist, the osteopath, to Amber's course in Feminist Literary Theory, to the gym for strength training. In between, Amber will write in her journal and talk to Joachim on the phone. Carnelia will unload the dishwasher, cook soup, and meditate. She will watch the snow swirl over the fir trees—Carnelia the snowy owl, Amber the baby crow, eating the black meat of winter. On the one year anniversary of the accident they dance to Bessie Smith, while Ari pours green tea from a purple teapot. Carnelia and Amber list the drugs Amber has taken and speak of how pain has its own fire echo, how the titanium burns. How she is metal woman, a bionic icon.

Eight years later at 4 a.m. Carnelia still hears Amber pleading for relief and returns to meditating.

Insomniac's List

Carnelia does not do sheep. She climbs the alphabet instead: autopsy, bacteria, colitis, diarrhea, electrocardiogram, etc. But then she's anxious over J. Nothing comes, except Jimmy fund. Is that cheating? What are the rules? She'd like to take it up with the author of sleep. She would say, *What do you want from me great Snoring Breath of Life that when I rise from bed I walk from room to room, staring out windows, like a cow into the snow?* Not even coffee can wind her up. Today she must take Amber to the orthopedic surgeon who will discuss the follow-up surgery on Amber's elbow. How will Carnelia focus on the X rays when the titanium loop with its screws and wires dismantles her? The doctor's bald head will shine like a lunatic's eyeball. "You've been through worse," she'll say to Amber, driving home, the bottom of her eye sockets aching from sleepless nights when the Almighty alphabet wraps around her like a python until dawn.

Ozone

The moon owns Carnelia. She is her slave, her "o gape."* It holds her, forbids her to sleep. Lidless, they stare at each other and into the dark ozone. The moon is white, licked clean bone, a red socket of a mastodon's femur head, that ball which Kali slices with her knives of fingers. Who can trust Carnelia with the simplest tasks when the moon boils red and white, leaving her with a taste of ash on her tongue and a distinct mistrust of the sun?

*Sylvia Plath, "The Moon and Yew Tree"

Fall Asleep

Ari likes to fall asleep, listening to opera overtures. Carnelia would never tell him it's a stupid idea. But when she's in bed and hears Verdi's overture to *Aida* she wants to jump up and march. Someone hands her a saber. Bonfires break out in shadows on the walls. Then she is Aida, gyrating down an obsidian staircase, cheetah skins covering her breasts, while Ari snores. But it's okay. She never sleeps much, anyway, busy remembering the faces of the dead: Pearl, her mother, Ruby and Beryl her aunts, their hands and feet. Often she's confused over whose feet match whose hands. Now she sees them in the procession, returning from Egypt, leading leopards and elephants with jeweled collars. Her mother lopes along on a camel, whose neck is strewn with iolite beads. Pearl is afraid people are looking up her skirt. But she waves and smiles, her hands supple and the color of peach roses. Her feet smooth against the beaded stirrups.

Titanium

This is the only way Carnelia and Amber meet now: when Carnelia turns the corner above the small houses and finds the crescent moon, demitasse of loss, jeweled blade of the Top Kapi palace, like the MRI of Amber's titanium pelvis. Amber lives in a city Carnelia does not know. The shock of the moon's crescent returning to Amber reminds her of pressing her head under Carnelia's jawbone, a tiny imprint leaving its honeyed fire.

Sushi

Ari loves sushi, sashimi. But Carnelia can never get past the raw. Still she adores the colors. The Avocado, like green parrot wings. The rabbit ear pink of salmon. She'll stick with the chive dumplings, the lovely shapes—babies' fists, falling and rising in sleep. She hopes Ari will drink enough sake to wash away his anger at Amber for leaving, then coming back broken. Her pain eats through him, though routinely he opens patients' jawbones, inserting his own titanium and creating prostheses that fit over them. Now the patient can chew again and feel human. Now Ari's staff cheers and Ari takes another maki. Carnelia knows this tamed rawness is deft death, eatable for only a few hours. But it excites Ari, though it will take Amber two years to heal and go on with her life. Meanwhile, Ari chews his sashimi. Carnelia drinks green tea.

Pleading Insanity

The cross dressing dermatologist was in a psychotic state when he shot his wife in the head. He hid in his sister's closet, inside her clothes, trying to escape their alcoholic father. All his life he struggled to appear normal. That's what his lawyer said, pleading insanity . . . Carnelia suddenly sees his wife's body giving into lead. Swans of blood spiral on the marble floor. How goodly are Thy tents, Oh Jacob, Thy dwelling places, Oh God of Mercy. The November sky is as gray as the fingers of the dead. A blue jay holds onto the empty branch of an oak. Its wings vibrate in the wind, feathery harps, accompanying the gnawing note it pierces the world with. Carnelia must find a parking space and teach a class while the dead woman is lodged in her third eye. The blue jay's stigmata of sound echoes in widening circles.

Empty Nest

Carnelia hasn't seen Amber in eight months—emails bounced back, calls unanswered. This was the child she prayed for, for whom she scrawled "Grant me a Child," tucking the paper in a crevice in the Wailing Wall. Nine months later her daughter was born, the daughter who writes better poetry than Carnelia, who adores Georgia O'Keeffe. Carnelia dreams a tiger chases Amber, her only escape through a ring of fire. Sweating, Carnelia wakes, her many selves calling to her, like the ocean to a woman who has stripped off her clothes. She must see the past as that crevice in the Wall. She must see herself as Amber, as the tiger. The hoop of fire.

Burgundy

Carnelia and Ari go to buy dog food. She sees the burgundy and blue Eclectus Parrot. Why would they have a stuffed bird here, all fluffed up, its colors from a fairy tale? When the sales rep. puts the parrot on her finger, it stretches out rainbow wings. Carnelia forgets her sorrow and brings the bird home. She calls her Burgundy and sings to her in the quiet of twilight. Burgundy sits on her shoulder and preens Carnelia's dark hair. Both of them stare out the window, lulled by the summer breeze, the two of them wrapped in the clean bandage of each other's emptiness. Each other's now.

Fire at the Hospitality Center

The fire trucks screech, like tortured cats, their lights spinning. Carnelia drives by the Culinary Institute's Hospitality Center on her way to work. She does not stop. A woman in a scorched chef's hat is sobbing on the curb. Carnelia can see flames licking the hospitality sign. Down the street someone is washing the giant rooster that stands in front of the Portuguese liquor store. After work Carnelia passes the smoldering building again. Poofs of soot shoot from the charred roof like frayed black flags over a used car lot. All night Carnelia dreams of the woman she did not stop for, who wore a purple babushka, like Carnelia's great aunt. The stranger stumbles around the underground cisterns of Istanbul where the giant carved head of Medusa lolls its snaky mane. Then she is dancing with fire, quite adept with the dos-à-dos. Next she turns into Amber, jumping through hoops of fire to escape the tiger chasing her. The next morning Carnelia pulls over, but there's no one there. Only rubble.

Red Radio Heart

Carnelia is tired of her heart. It's too heavy. When she tries to sleep it bumps, then races. She pictures it, disentangling itself from the system that feeds it, then shrinking, escaping out of her mouth, rolling down the street. Sticky candy apple heart. Road kill heart. She could have a pig's heart. Or a red radio heart that would play jazz for her but not Bartok. Her heart in a yellow basket that Ella Fitzgerald has lost. Maybe Frankenstein will stagger out from behind the billboard that supports the war. He'll need a new heart, too. Maybe he'll scoop up hers and she'll be free of her clumsy overripe blood orange heart. Meanwhile, the generals beef up attacks.

Ventricles

That black bird devours Carnelia's heart a piece each day, but it still beats. So does the bird's, whose wings fold over snow, like black lava. Amber's absence set the bird on Carnelia. How is Amber's heart? Hardened to candy apple lacquer? The winter extends itself and by spring Carnelia's heart will be gone. But Amber's will thaw and open like a poppy whose opiates do not float on the wind but sink deeper into it.

Red chambers. Fire alone names you, Amber. Carnelia signing off. Iced.

"Sludge"

Carnelia emailed her therapist an S.O.S. on New Year's Eve. For two weeks Carnelia waited for an answer, each day sinking farther down on the black rungs of her black ladder. She stared out the kitchen window in her bathrobe watching the sun burst flamingo. Watching the purple cinders of dawn split open like torn ligaments. All her failings flooded her, all the betrayals. Even Amber couldn't get far enough away. What had Carnelia's life come to? Paying a therapist to ignore her. Raising a daughter who turns away. When Carnelia's rejected poems came back, she was still in her bathrobe. The snow started to cover a milk bottle stuffed with a black note on the front stoop. Carnelia longed for magenta dahlias, big as dinner plates, Ari digging in the flower beds and Amber reciting poetry on the porch. There was nothing but the white swan of snow spreading its wings against the black swan of emptiness. Nothing but Carnelia willing herself upstairs into the bathtub, the hot water calming her. She pictured water rushing from the drain to the sewer, the sewer to the treatment plant. Her sweat and oils turned to sludge. This will be the title of her students' next poems. "Sludge."

Part Two

❋ ❋ ❋

"I've eaten a bag of green apples,
Boarded the train there's no getting off."

From "Metaphors"
by Sylvia Plath

Louie Loves Kids

When Carnelia's father Louie was seventy the neighborhood boy still knocked at the door. "Can Woowie come out and pway?" Louie went out and threw the yellow foam football right into the kid's cupped hands, while pink and blue streamers scrambled the late august sky. Carnelia and her mother stared through the kitchen window. "He's so good with kids. It's adults he can't take," Pearl said, scrubbing the roasting pan harder. Mostly he told his bosses off, drifting from mutual funds, to insurance, to used cars. Carnelia remembered the used car lot with the plastic flags jerking in the wind. Louie standing there like a king reduced to jesterhood. He graduated from law school, but never practiced. When he came home, Pearl was right on him, saying, "Did you sell any cars today?"

His three daughters worshipped him but the young couple from Puerto Rico sure didn't. They bought a '59 Rambler from Louie for $300 that gave out a week later in the parking lot of their apartment house. The couple cursed Louie en Español, and Carnelia had to get a waitressing job to pay for gas and chocolate. When Carnelia decided to be a poet, Louie said, "Somebody has to write the poems. Why shouldn't it be you?"

Carnelia keeps dreaming of those red and blue flags, their riotous, ragged sweeps against the throbbing sky. She dreams of Louie's dingy desk in the corner of the car lot inside a tent set up for the G.W. sale, his freezing hand gripping a Bic over the sales contract, the handshakes, Louie's gin thick in the freezer. The ghost of him now still sick of adults, still playing ball with the young ones, who have just made it to the other side.

Pastrami

Carnelia loves buying food. She strides out of the deli with two bags, moves on to the bakery. She has never felt so alive, although she's just come from her Uncle's funeral. She wept with her sisters Opal and Jade over their parents' graves, their Uncles' and Aunts'. Then they hit the deli where Romanian pastrami struck like gypsies' tambourines over Carnelia's tongue. Opal ate French toast, soft against her tongue that was sore from the lesion they removed. Jade had lean corned beef on rye, their father Louie's favorite. When they said prayers for Uncle Harry, they were standing on burlap that covered their parents' graves. The cemetery had horizontal plaques, not tombstones. They had always been careful not to step on those markers, sweeping off the leaves, placing flowers around the names.

It was a dream sequence: the wind, the canopy, everyone throwing earth on the casket, the burlap underneath it along with their parents' names underneath and the femurs that had run with them. The ulnas that held them. The skulls singing the white song of the grave that has no sound but never ceases.

When they drive to their cousin's house, Carnelia isn't sure how they will take her. But they are welcoming, as if at a party that will never end. Although she didn't know her cousins, they are real in their grief. She keeps drinking scotch, studying their children, seeing the flint of their great grandparents skipping through each eye. Next the long drive home with Opal. The endless old stories remembered so differently by each sister. Now the exhaustion, as if Carnelia has been pounded and roasted in a slow oven over night. Carnelia with her high cholesterol, a giant walking mound of Romanian pastrami, cured tender. The old toughness gone.

Greens

Carnelia's ankles are swollen, her stomach full, like she's carrying dead twins. Nothing helps. The nutritionist pats a plastic four ounce Chicken breast in her hand. Carnelia tells her to forget the chicken, forget the vegetables and lemon juice. She remembers an old friend who used to say her favorite green vegetable was green M&Ms. Carnelia knows she never wants to hear the nutritionist's nasal tones again. Or gaze at the plastic Big Mac on her desk with the 2,000 calorie label underneath. No. She will get into her car and listen to jazz, which will dissolve the food expert's grim face, that just now reminds her of her mother's. She will go home, the thought of chicken still gagging her, have a whole wheat bagel with low fat cream cheese and a glass of white wine.

X-rays Reveal Severe Arthritis of Both Knees

Alone with her bones, Carnelia remembers her body in the crib.
She rippled Va-Va-Va-Va. The rhythm of her limbs, her viscera
hum-singing, not the current stinging, but the pelvic tilt of infancy.
Sunlight floods the bedroom, white curtains swimming to her croon.
Outside the door, the low pitch, the high pitch. "She's cooing."
Really, Carnelia was floating on waves of her own biosphere:
smooth muscle, clean bone, tendons. Pea vines climbing. And her
heart, that tiny red dragon, rising, sinking in the theatre of her chest.
Until darkness crept into her and those swaying curtains blacked
out. She can still remember someone's fingers, lace sweeping down
her face. Then the quiver of arrows, bow of silence.

Laser Spine Surgery: 8 Days Post-Op

Carnelia is walking for herself and for those who cannot walk—the dead, whose legs of dust support her, and the living, lying in gauze, watching their own embalming. She has risen from the rubble of her bones, lasered, glistening. Minus nerve endings, shaved disc dust. She wavers in her white velcro back brace, a black and white cow staggering in a field, devoured by moonlight. She clomps forward, swinging her arms, once monster-like but now forming a winged arc. These legs that failed her, that stung and went numb, start to talk to the ground. It says go, complete the sweet equation Euclid knew, whose mind out-walked his body in pure cosmic momentum. All biomechanics make sense to Carnelia, now striding, buffered by the moon and the North Star. Her dead parents, chanting in the cold cockpits of her vertebrae. Her breath heaving, "Halleluiah."

The Death of the King of the Gypsies

The only way Carnelia meets her father Louie now is in the improv of Coltrane's sax. Its jack rabbit jumps, its limbos dissolving into the purple orchid sunset.

Driving home, she sees Louie's black eyebrows in the kamikaze strokes of sundown. She hears his honey gravel voice in the low dip of the sax that falls off the cliff of itself at the end of "Naima." Louie fell off his cliff twenty years ago. She keeps waiting for him to show up after midnight in a spinning web of ice and tell her how it's going. She remembers shoveling dirt onto his coffin—a good deed to help him rest in the dust.

But Louie doesn't come. Instead Carnelia remembers stroking his forehead, feeling his shock of thick white hair as he gripped her hand through another day of morphine. His blind eye shone white, like a marble rolled back in his head where he discovered a black cave with painted horses, martini glasses and lovers tangled in midnight briar. She sang him "Moonlight in Vermont," then pulled herself away to pick up Amber, his only granddaughter.

After Opal and Carnelia chose his coffin and his suit and tie, after the chapel and the mourners, the speeches and the poems, the cemetery and the El Moleh Rachamim, the Kaddish, the boiled eggs and the schnapps and cream cheese and bagels, they took down the old photographs and left his apartment empty, except for two rubber tipped canes. Then the afternoons turned long because there was no one to listen to Ella with, no one encouraging her to go home and feed her family.

Just remembering how Louie took pain knocks Carnelia out. How he thanked the nurses for cleaning him. This man who threw a piano out a hotel window with his friends one night because they didn't like the music, who stood in his pink Bermuda shorts in Miami in the summer of 1956, blasting the Cuban station from his Chevy, teaching Carnelia Cha Cha moves, who went bankrupt filling his customers' oil tanks, collecting only what they could pay.

Carnelia pictures his oil truck "Mercury Heat" with the figure of the winged god painted on the side. How she waited for those huge tires to gouge the gravel driveway, how he scooped her up into the cabin and let her steer on his lap.

It was Louie scrubbing himself into cleanliness before dinner, discussing the day's news, making each daughter explain something she'd noticed or learned. It was Louie who'd do anything for his friends but cursed his enemies, while sipping martinis, watching old John Wayne movies.

It's this highway jazz that still laces Louie to Carnelia. The asphalt's swaying, while the sun burns out in flayed salmon streaks that precede the fountain of black emeralds showering us down to the grave. She and Louie are hovering around each other in the streaming raucous nonchalance of jazz. He's in her breathing, in her name. In the quiet shrine of dreams of finding him just around the corner.

Sleep

Sleeps' fingers smooth Carnelia, caressing away grief when she rises from the catacombs of repose. She remembers her dream of hiding from soldiers inside mountain clefts where stored tombs rest. Carnelia staggers, stretches her cramped muscles and recomposes her spine. In a steaming shower her bruises sing to her, a barn swallow, serenading a slave. She searches for swirls of satin through each fading ruby dawn. All day she waits to stretch out when purples split the surimi skin of sundown. "You are mine," she says to sleep. "Your fingers sway over the harp of my body. Sweet spring water. Sleep, you are my dead sister, erasing the face of my accuser."

Hospice

Carnelia cannot negotiate the cavernous silence of Opal's death. Even though Opal could not speak, she wrote everything down until her strength failed. Then Carnelia wrote everything down. When Opal lay in the hospice bed in her flowered smock, she was so alive, her eyes vivid, her gestures large. When Jade arrived the three sisters sat there, staring at the blue hydrangea Jade brought. Opal managed to write in her last burst, "What other blues?" Jade and Carnelia described blue blankets they had all slept under, the turquoise blue of their mother's eyes. Carnelia wrote a whole list of blues that night: angora sweater, ocean, old Orchard beach Maine in noon sun, etc. But the next day when Carnelia got there with Opal's husband and youngest son, Opal was limp, her breaths slow. Gull wing slow, arching over the pier into the swelling waves.

Gladiator

Carnelia's sister Opal said, "Follow me. You will write about this."
She sprang into the radiation room, Carnelia behind her. Opal
spouted Latin poetry. Ovid, love in the face of death. She hopped
onto the table and the technician pressed a white Hockey mask
over her face, the grids marking her. He pressed the button and the
machine gave her all it had. When it was over Opal jumped off and
finished reciting the poem. She thanked him for his good work,
then got dressed and reminded Carnelia to get her parking ticket
stamped. She led Carnelia through the bowels of the hospital.
Opal insisted she was fine to drive home, that Carnelia should go
to work, which she did. Dazed. When Opal got home she blasted
Aretha Franklin, dancing in the living room. When Carnelia called
that night, Opal said it had been a good day.

Lamb's Head

Carnelia vows to stop watching cooking shows, especially ones about Lebanese food, about spinal cord boiled, then simmered in a sauce and served in a sandwich. She watches a man in a yellow T-shirt nibbling on the pieces of spinal cord, his eyes rolling like a lover's. His jaw works furiously as the juice drips from his mouth, then the camera close-up of a lamb's head. The chef is saying that his customers, all men, come once or twice a week for cord and head. "It's very labor intensive. First you have to boil them, throw out the clotted water, spice the next water bath with cardamom and bay leaf, dip them in egg, flour. Then bread them. Next you roast them for three to four hours." Finally, the head sits on the platter, like a cartoon of John the Baptist.

Another man sits waiting, sweating, his eyes glaring, his red shirt clinging to his belly that looks like a sausage. He plunges his fork into the left temple of the lamb's head, then lifts his knife. Carnelia feels her colon convulse as he chews and wags his head. Now he goes for an eyeball, plucking it from its socket with his fingers. When he puts it into his mouth, music swells and the camera zigzags as if the technician can bear no more.

Several days later Carnelia's student, Nadine, stays after class to ask questions. When Nadine speaks of phallocentricism and women's silence, all Carnelia can think of is a lamb's head on Nadine's shoulders—its bold black eyes, flat nose, and long jaw. Carnelia will never watch another cooking show and she lacks the courage to ask Nadine if in Lebanon her grandmother prepared these foods. "Professor, you look faint," Nadine says, retrieving a chair for her and a bottle of water. Nadine thinks its hypoglycemia. But of course it's not.

dew

Voices come to Carnelia as she wakes. For instance dew's. "I am the crying jag of creation," dew whispers, "I depose the roses' sleep with dawn's blood. My wet jag daggering tight blooms. You can wash your feet, in my cool pearls, prepare yourself for the fires of noon." How can Carnelia explain to anyone that this is her religion?

Wedding

Amber wants to marry a tree. She likes the way her skin feels against its bark. The softness of its leaves. She likes the way its branches hold her and its low moans in the wind. "Tree, tree, will you marry me?" Every day she repeats her proposal. One day its leaves are burning scarlet, molten gold, and ambushes of orange rush out at her. She takes this as the Tree's yes. Her parents hire a caterer, a klezmer band, a pagan rabbi. They even have little match books printed that say "Amber and Tree." On the day of the ceremony at Tree's park, the weather turns bitter and Tree's leaves flail in a staggering wind. The wedding guests step on them and they crack. Not even the klezmeren can drown out the sound. Amber sobs. Carnelia and Ari motion for everyone to go home. Meanwhile, Tree stands naked, xylem, phloem, urgent, surging. Centuries of broken violins play gypsy melodies, hurling themselves up through its roots. Each night Amber dreams of butterflies alighting on Tree's bark, turning to fire. Absence has its own language that seeps underground. Wild music fills them both.

They will not live to spring.

Scorched

Carnelia goes into a florist's to buy a plant for a friend, a recent widow. It smells like an overactive oil burner, a smell from her childhood. Her father was in the oil business when ten-year-old Carnelia answered the phone. "Mercury Heat. May I help you? Oh it's you Mrs. Doyle. Your furnace died? Have you pressed the reset button? Go press it. Let me know what happens." Carnelia looks around for an Xmas cactus, or a Dutch shoe with holes where tulip bulbs will shoot out. Nothing, just scathed oil. Now she sees the plants are all dead. The pothos droop like dead lambs' ears wrapped in spider webs. The florist comes out from the back room, all apologies. "The boiler exploded. The heat died. We've lost all the plants." Carnelia stares at his hands that look like mottled white rubber. There are raspberry stains over his wrists. A burn patient, she thinks. He has no luck. "I'll come again," she says, closing the door. She drives by but never stops.

Carnelia Doesn't Get Relief from Acupuncture
But She Gets This List:

birdcalls   nesteggs   beachfeathers

horsenays   coltstumbles   petfood

beessucks   roseblooms   driedblood

ironore   fireforge   handcuffs

justnow   morebreath   letgo

Egg Dream

Carnelia's egg dream is disturbing her, not that she can retrieve it all. Something about standing at the stove cracking eggs. But they wouldn't drop in the bowl. They drooled over the side, oozing like bad music. And, oh no, Mr. Woodbind, her neighbor, was standing behind her, bleeding from the back of his ankles. His blood pooled around her feet. It was sticky when she looked down. She saw she was naked. Should she grab the paring knife, pivot? Or should she stand there, listening to the eggs? They had just started singing the "Our Father" in Latin when she woke up. Her head ached, her feet sweaty, like someone had cracked her open. She bled yoke all day until she discovered herself standing at Mr. Woodbind's door with a chocolate soufflé. A treat for a widower.

The History of Carnelia's Body

A black fish with a feather tail hissed through the yellow center of my eye. I began to grow until I burst. Through the groans, the cold, I learned to hate what I did to her. To love the flames my lungs bellowed out. She forgave me but I was of two minds: one to furrow back into her, another to leap beyond her stroking.

Carnelia reads these old words she scrawled when Amber was an infant. They are her own birthmark, or bookmark, and Amber's. Also the account of her own birth.

Her thighs have not changed. They are not somber or frail. They are inner tubes of floating islands she sets her course by. They pull her through humid space, or keep her spellbound in the frigid air, dispelling ice, like stoves.

Flash falls of plumes swoon down, deep inside her rib cage. Even now, white pinions cover her. Her breasts are towering peonies, opening. They have sunk low, edges of their blossoms, deep pink to brown.

Tigris bloods her. Her hands are fixtures of silt, her feet appendices of sludge. Her behind has remained in its own class, trailing after the rest of her. Landscape of snow mounds where round faces stare into caves of sleeping white bears.

In her brain there is a deep cleft. On one side the sun fills the valleys where sheep graze. On the other, a deep ravine descends where black snakes swarm in dank bayous. Beware that mud. Out-stare that stare.

Pray to the cauldron of her stomach that churns skins and seeds.

Bow to her ovaries, those bowls of stars. And also to her womb from which a genius spun out, bawling, crushed by cold air and the iron lung of gravity. The closed down womb, now a museum piece.

Consider her tongue, raw flamingo of the triptych of her throat, the cravings that rise up. Cossacks on horseback, banging down the door, their spurs still dig into their sides.

The Chagall windows of her blue and purple veins stun her calves and the back of her left knee with a deep reverie, spreading.

Darling toes and ankle bones, tarsal, metatarsal. Your wide patience sustains her. Only her fingers are as loyal, flailing, and trailing words, like music through the air for emphasis.

Gale winds bring her back to her heart, whose red isolation rises beyond the clamped throb of its own hammer. Stay awhile inside the tattoo parlor of drums you boom through. These words swim free because of you and the centipede bridges of her brain.

Her mouth still plucks the other's mouth, tangos him into her naked discontent. Her body bears its history of clots and disso-nance.

It is her own treatment center for the addiction of living, of breath and water, her body a city succumbing to desert and flood, still poised against the echoes of battery.

Holy body of Carnelia's blood.

Naked City

The narrator says, "Every murder turns on a white hot light that detectives follow, like a rope uncoiling from a hanging." "The Naked City," circa 1940 with Barry Fitzgerald as the police captain. Carnelia has taken to mid morning movies in the smashed-bone fatigue of Epstein Barr. At least her mind can follow a plot, detect a murderer. The victim is 26, a red-haired beauty, whose mother hates her for changing her name, until she sees her daughter's corpse and sobs, "Baby, my Baby, my Baby." This makes Carnelia remember Amber in the tub—bubbles blowing from her pink bow mouth, her peach fuzz hair meringued with shampoo. Amber is the same age as the daughter on TV. Not dead but estranged. Carnelia cringes while Barry's brogue seduces the mother into handing over the victim's diary. The parents think she was a model in L.A., not a porn star. Amber's diary, no doubt, is full of disgust for her parents. Her poems are Molotov cocktails. Carnelia falls asleep before guessing the murderer. She dreams that she and Ari are at the train station, Amber standing in front of the open doors. Ari freezes as Carnelia runs to embrace their daughter, who is calm and dressed in purple, an iris floating. When Carnelia wakes, she is still half pressed to Amber, prying Ari off the tracks.

Isis

Carnelia is watching the PBS documentary on pigs for the third time. She is waiting for the part when Carol somewhere in California adopts thirty abandoned pigs and makes a little village for them out of cardboard box huts, along with bedding. There are toddler wading pools filled with pigs. Carol explains that pet store owners lied to people in the '80s, claiming that the piglets, if fed a half a cup of feed a day, would not exceed 25 pounds. But Great Expectations, her own pig is a good 325 pounds. All the others are up there too. Why couldn't those people figure out that pigs wouldn't settle for half a cup? So Carol takes them in, scrubs, chides and consoles them. She walks by the ocean with pigs following her, snorting. It makes Carnelia cry. But now there's a part she's never seen: the narrator's voice, a man's, discusses why Jews and Muslims consider pork unclean. He says it's the disease pigs carry. Or that in ancient times they could not be herded. Suddenly Carnelia is standing, yelling at the screen. "The pig was sacred to Isis. Tell the truth!" Anyone who studied the transition of Mother Goddess worship to the patriarchal gods knows this. But even PBS is keeping it all a secret. She'd like to let Carol know. She smiles, thinking that at least the pigs know Carol is the reincarnation of Isis.

Artemis of Ephesus

Carnelia and Ari take a jeep down the King's Road running through the Anatolian plateau to reach Sousa—the road through the Kaistros valley to Sardis, the Romans' safest trade route. They find Ephesus, the harbor where the sun sears down over the same bartering that preceded the Pax Romana. They climb the mountain to find the Temple of Artemis Ephesia. Only her statue is left in the museum.

Carnelia breathes in the heavy summer air. The clouds are chiseled columns breaking back through centuries, she enters the sanctuary. The Goddess stands on a massive pedestal, two deer, two bee hives attend her feet. She is immense, reaching out to Carnelia. Her crown has three tiers: the top a temple, the bottom two, her sacred lions, goats, deer, and panthers. Carnelia kneels to keep from falling. Never has she knelt before a divine image until now.

Here the Goddess' massive neck is covered with molded pearls, precious stones, bunches of grapes. From her torso protrude dozens of egg orbs, or breasts, or bull balls. They are her armor. More sacred animals adorn her skirt, and as Carnelia approaches the altar, she sees two Muses holding flutes to their mouths, calling to her from the stone. She can hear the Goddess breathing, waves hurling to shore. Carnelia places garlands and pomegranates on the white marble, also herbs and incense, an urn of honey. She bows her head, setting down the last offering of white eggs.

Many other women join her, making the same offerings. Now they chant "Mother of Ripening of all that Grows, the fields, the honey, the honey comb, the bulls' testes, the bellies of cows, the red rinds of fruit, their dark seeds. All that swells from your body, let that fullness be ours. Let your sacred bees surround us. No other

Mother thickens the honey. We are your daughters, fruit of your womb. Touch us with your ripeness. Free us from blood without fullness. Give us your pulse. Set your fire in us. We will not forsake you, Magna Mater."

Ari tells Carnelia she has stayed too long in the oven of the museum. She stumbles down the mountain and sees white papers tied around bushes. Ari says they are prayers written today and left for the wind. Carnelia hears and is infused in those prayers. "Great Mother of Anatolia, I have entered your temple. Part of me is buried under the scanthus leaves of those who dethroned you."

Red Orchids

When Carnelia bled she bled red orchids, crimson ribbons, tiny strangled corpses. She couldn't get enough salt or sugar. Anything fried she tied to her sides. She bulged. She shrank. She danced the full moon dance, like any native red-blooded bleeder. Then she waited for the eggs and felt them plummet. She washed and drove to work, accelerating with each spasm. Insomnia overtook her, like the moon over the desert. Her eyes were lidless moons and she saw the movie of desire, stretching like a canvas under acids that devour the painter, as well as the paint. The "Ovoid of (my)darkness"* caressed her. Then the sun performed surgery on itself, parting the flesh of the sky into T-bone red streaks. Someone said, "Make me an omelet." How can an omelet make an omelet?

Then after decades the lava came up from her depths. Scalded, she ran to the window of the classroom and ripped it open, shoving her head out, *Snow storm after snow storm*, as the students eyed her. After her father died, she stopped bleeding for nine months. But the blood eventually returned. The waiting was like listening for music when the orchestra has been gassed. Now it's more like a cavern of buried sacrifice. The sea and the wind pound out rhythms of old women, whose cave paintings remain in her. Bird droppings, amulets of tourmaline, the bald eye of the moon, all inside her. Sometimes she dreams of those women. They tell her to break her silence, to honor the Mother from whom we were pulled in the cauldrons of our births. Carnelia doesn't sleep much now, trying to stare from a high place into the face of this Mother.

* Sylvia Plath, "The Moon and the Yew Tree"

A Jew in Cairo

Carnelia and Ari are staying in Cairo at a hotel on the Nile. Four weeks ago she had a sarcoma the size of a baseball removed from the center of her chest, but she insisted on travelling. How many more trips do she and Ari have? Her scar sings a spinning gypsy song to her of blades and violins. She has vowed to have only one adventure each day, to rest, then accompany Ari to dinner.

This late afternoon she is reading Leila Ahmed on the patio when the muezzins begin their prayer. Their voices, hibiscus soaked, spiral into the sunset. Wheels of rose gold explode into flames, singeing blue streaks of sky that pulse like tendons in the wings of the Angel Gabriel.

Four white birds fly by, reminding Carnelia to return to her body.

When she bows her head, the muezzins' voices ignite in her. She has a God rush, the God who forgives her for scratching in the ashes of her own annihilation. She forgives herself for having turned away. The prayer rises from the supplicants' intestines, then rolls over the sky, ballooning down into the Nile, into Nassar's silt, into today's filth. Then it revives and sails back into the light. Anubis the jackal lifts it from the mud.

Four white birds fly by, reminding Carnelia to return to her body.

Still the voices of all the muezzins anoint her. A silk worm spinning strands of gold, enfolding her over and over. Carnelia, a breathing mummy, restored from her own embalming.

Four white birds fly by, reminding Carnelia to revere her body.

Her bones are now lutes. Her heart is newly wrapped, it is fixed and fired in the oven of the sun, replaced in her body by the black glove of the moon. To Carnelia, all of Creation is now the one voice of the people adoring the Creator, swaying above the sirens, tearing the air into twisted metal. A surgeon's hand reached inside Carnelia, blading out the cancer, saving her for this moment.

Four white birds fly by, reminding Carnelia to chant the Blessing: "Blessed art Thou, our G-d who gives us life, who sustains us and has brought us to this day."

PART THREE

✻ ✻ ✻

"In the first farm I stopped at I found some partisans.
I was much too exhausted to join them. All I recalled
is that I slept for two days and nights under a thick,
flower covered comforter, and that a woman made me
drink hot milk."

From *Days and Memory*
by Charlotte Delbo
Translated by Rosette Lamont

Carnelia Interrogates Sex and Gender

If Woman is a fluid category and if language extends from the Symbolic Order, the Law of the Father, then is Carnelia a woman? Or many women? Is she a man in a woman's body? Or in the words of St. Thomas Aquinas, a "misbegotten male?" Perhaps she is androgynous with her long clitoris, shoulders like a boxer's. She can press two hundred pounds. But still she is supposed to show cleavage in eveningwear. She had very talkative ovaries when they worked. They screeched out little "why me's?" as the menstrual cramps ratcheted tighter. For the sake of simplicity or reductionism, let's say she's a woman, but has certain insight concerning the penis. Not penis envy but genital weight.

How she performs her gender? She learned from Annette Funicello to act dumb and smile, from Elizabeth Taylor, to roll her eyes and suck in her gut. Still after menopause, she paints her fingernails and colors her hair, though she's always railing against a misplaced emphasis on youth and physical beauty. She professes feminism but is a fake. If she sold her jewelry she could feed Sudan. But she needs those diamonds in case the Fourth Reich goose steps in.

She acts like her father at times, who pulled the car over and puked after four martinis, then went on driving. She knows how to argue and make a case for her ideas. She loves words and the power of convincing others. Is that gender? Her mother swooned over nubby purple fabric, lemon-yellow and robin's egg blue. Carnelia does all that, too, so is that gender performance?

As a hippie she had a purple and orange striped dress with a belt of bells. When the knighted poet called her she went to his hotel. His jaw was a crag in a rock where mountain goats scrambled. She caressed that jaw. Her bells rippled in the air of honey and scotch. But after two wives' suicides he could not perform.

When she married Ari she was 27. They did not want children, but her clock did more than tick. How much was that hard wiring, the desire to have a daughter who would exceed her in looks and smarts? How much of it was doom disguised as love? Love as doom? Maybe it was her left handedness, her inability to get Amber's socks on straight that left her exhausted. No necklace in the world made Carnelia feel gorgeous. No class she prepared was prepared well enough. No dinner she cooked was elegant enough. Ari lost his temper and the rest is Amber's story, who tells it her own way.

Carnelia still dresses in bright colors, she changes her rings daily and twirls her hands in supine gestures. This week's nail polish is "Your Private Jet"—a grey lacquer with sparkles.

Carnelia Interrogates Religion

I.

Carnelia's a big hit at the Catholic College. She's an accommodating Jew. But is she really Jewish? "You Rosenblatt," Ellis Island officials told her maternal grandfather. "Skournig translates into skinner or tanner," Grandfather said. But they stamped him "Rosenblatt." Her mother Pearl changed it to Rawsen to get a job. *Try not to let them know you're Jewish on the outside. Just be Jewish on the inside.*

The Rabbi at Hebrew School where the boys hated smart girls said to put your hand in the empty box. What was in the box? Atoms, neutrons, even God was there. But you couldn't see Him/ Her/ It. Carnelia wanted God, but not an old man with a white beard, not a Grandfather who would not let women read from the Torah because they might be bleeding secret blood. So she prayed, "Dear Ferris Wheel of Nuclear Power."

Carnelia remained the outsider. She could not take the Confirmation oath in the Synagogue. "I consecrate myself to my People and to my People's Faith." She could not say it, sixteen, breathing in Walt Whitman. She could not believe in a God who asked a parent to kill his child. Then when her father Louie went bankrupt and couldn't pay Synagogue membership, Carnelia had to work as a gift wrapper. She remembered the women at the synagogue with their diamonds and mink stoles, circling the congregation, looking to see who was wearing what, while the Rabbi's hands shook in his sermon, his voice merging with the stained glass windows' purple light.

When she met Ari, she wanted her own narrative. She consented to keep a kosher home. But her mother planned a wedding mixing dairy with meat, an insult to her future in-laws. Ari and Carnelia married in the Rabbi's study with no family, only two witnesses. He broke the glass with his heel, to remember the destruction of the Second Temple, which marriage rebuilds.

As newlyweds they flew to Amsterdam right after the ceremony. On returning, her parents welcomed them with pursed lips.

Now with Amber turning away, all the teachings of the sages are so many pages from a coloring book. There was nothing in the sacred book about healing the deep patriarchal wound. Yet when Carnelia hears the old melodies, she's still that young woman dressed all in white for Yom Kippur, thanking the burning bush God, remembering how she pushed that note in the crack of the Wailing Wall that read, "Grant me a child."

Carnelia Interrogates Religion

2.

What is the point of denying the Holy One? Someone has to teach the students about the Holocaust because the first one to ask Carnelia for an independent study said she'd never heard of it. Now they are all reaching for God, for sanity and for each other. It changes how they see themselves. Can they imagine how one raspberry tastes when you are starving? Will their dreams consume them with those clawing to stay alive?

Carnelia feels the mouths of the dead, blood clotted, earth packed, trying to swallow. When she reads Paul Celan's "Sound-dead sister shell,/ let the dwarf-sounds come in," they come in, choking her. Then they hold her up to speak of the unspeakable. No God would design a gas chamber or conveyer belts for burning corpses. So God must have been away, suffering. Some moments there is a closeness, a wisp of hair touching her face, a memory of the opposite of annihilation. Most of the time it is the injustice that drives her, Isaiah burning in the deep cursed breathing of her insomnia. Carnelia is a Neo-Judaic-Trapeze artist, forcing herself through the ash filled air, landing to say that some love survives. Even if she sometimes doubts it.

Carnelia Interrogates Race

Because race and gender are social constructions, because Jews were not considered white until the 1960s, because Carnelia never felt white with her olive skin and kinky hair and a nose that touched her upper lip when she smiled—because of all of these things, when Carnelia hears the black scholar of civil rights, the woman who shows the Powerpoint post cards of public hangings in the 1920s while whites picnicked and bands played on, Carnelia decides she will never check the white box on the questionnaires again. She remembers Harold Smith in fourth grade. He was mixed race, cocoa, scabs all over his bald head from medical treatments. He teetered on the stone embankment walking her home, pretending he was falling or about to fly, singing the whole time a song about the teacher who Carnelia years later realized resembled Queen Victoria in her mourning period for Prince Albert. She could abide no noise or humor. Harold and Carnelia were sent to the principal for laughing out loud, for falling off their chairs. Carnelia's mother disapproved of Harold, would not allow him into the duplex. Now Carnelia wants to know how long Harold kept singing. How many more treatments he withstood after he moved away.

The Fall of Leningrad

Carnelia listens to National Public Radio, the anniversary of the fall of Leningrad. She hears: "They sold their diamonds for bread when there was no bread left. They starved to death with trinkets under their pillows." She hears: *Sold diamonds bread. Starved. Dead trinkets pillows. Dead diamonds. Under starved. Left for death when there was no. They. They. They.* Carnelia skins a bulbous eggplant, cutting her finger, the Eyes of the Dead presiding over her kitchen.

Rubber

So Buna means rubber. The Nazis intended that the prisoners of Buna make rubber. But it never happened. Liberation came too soon. A few chemists survived, a few procurers. Now the word is a truncheon. It strikes a blow across your ear. A strap wrapped around the back of a chain linked hand whacks you. But you are only dreading Buna, hearing the blocked, shrieks of the dead.

just

another corpse flung on the corpse-pile another body flung onto
the conveyer swallowed by the maw of fire spit out as ash another
billow of rancid smoke choking the sky the lungs of those just
arriving what is that stench another lice-raging one dreaming of
soap and water meat and vegetables of clean sheets and underwear
now frozen stacked thawed burned disgorged into the belching soot
that cannot be washed off scoured out revised now reconstituted
as fertilizer they sweep through the atmosphere they seep into the
ground the turnips and potatoes take them in to swell for harvest
they make your stew delicious someone's parents' organs still steep
the fields sweeten the beets just another transport with the earth
still spinning around a dead sun a sun choked on gasses and silence
that enter the morning shafts of light these last atoms of the dead
creation splits open just another baby impaled on a bayonet why
waste a bullet just just just just just just just just just

Natzweiler:
The European Centre on Resistance and Deportation

Carnelia remembers the account of a Holocaust victim's mother, staring at the moon, picturing her daughter swaying from a gallows like the vacant ones Carnelia saw at the KL Natzweiler Camp. In Struthoff, outside of Strasbourg, the ropes still hang on the side of a hill above the white crosses down in the valley. Where are the stars of David? Way in the back behind the crematorium, behind the vast figure of Christ there is a small garden of posies and weeds. Someone has placed small stones over the plot. A small plaque refers to the Jews, no mention of "The Final Solution." Only the long lines of students laugh as they get off the buses until they reach the chamber of gas, then the crematorium next with its oven made of stones, the photo of one teenage girl in its gaping mouth. Carnelia watched all the students, their faces folding in. She walked around the crematorium, staring at the whips and hooks.

Those daughters, ropes slung over their heads, hands bound. What did they last picture, their mothers' hands, their fathers' eyes? She wants to remember all the dead, but what do the students go back with? The Jews still hidden away in ghettos of ash?

The Discovery Channel

The villagers refused to move the sacred bird from the ruined house, as Carnelia and Ari lay naked, decoding the velvet of each other's rainforests. Then the villagers descended precipices into valleys strewn with cerulean statues of the Black Madonna. There is no telling how long they cut through vines wider than lions' tails. A mongoose screech ripped through the mist-heavy crevices of the mahogany tree. When they returned to scheduled programming, the villagers had taken the wooden bird, the giant ladles, the drum, to a culture house anthropologists made for the village's artifacts. Smearing their faces with the blue juice of berries, the elders covered themselves in leaves and hung long strands of grass from their waist cinchers. They were chanting, dancing, swinging wicker wings skyward.

In the morning when Carnelia made the bed, under the covers she found blue juice stains. Wicker splinters scattered the floor.

Vintner

Carnelia did not understand his speech but understood his mouth, that it was a trough of dark wine. That all the grapes from his vines, the vines of his father and his grandfather were eviscerated there into pulp. Then from pulp they were pressed into juice, the skins and seeds sliding off for musky compost. He knew the secrets of the vats, how much pressure, what temperatures to bouquet juice into wine. She did not understand his words, but his hands passed the yellow compost over hers, like ground monarch butterflies. He wanted her to feel the dust of grape skin, seed, vine that he pressed into her fingers. She felt the grapes before they were ground up, rain riveted, driven in clusters that catch the light before being plucked, snagged, pulverized, heated, aged, bottled, labeled, "Apremont." She sat with him, and he pointed to the map, his mountains and he traced a timeline of erosion with his fingertips. His talk was ruby orchids, whose body glowed through his bones, as they drank wine together, toasting the grapes and sodden field. Then Ari arrived with the car.

The Costume Party

Is anybody home? Carnelia wraps her throat in pearls, stares into the mirror, seeing empty pits where her eyes used to be. The spiteful moon's black humor bores her, but Carnelia knows her secret, that white witch cut out her own tongue because she was tired of casual supplication. Carnelia wishes that a bird of paradise would drive its blood blossoms through the moon's heart of alabaster, penetrate her epiglottis of frozen milk, blister it black. Such contempt and utter devotion are not incompatible in the cupola of Carnelia's throbbing brain, to which the moon's polished hood of bone seems closer, more brilliant than any visitor downstairs.

The Perfect Mask

Carnelia in the mask shop in Venice wears the Venetian Columbine, the purple lips of the malicious maid. Black seeping eyes splash down in scorpions' tails across the porcelain cheeks. She also wears the black velvet of the moretta. The caul of the gnaga adorns the bone of her skull, and in these remnants of the Commedia Dell Arte she catches a glimpse of the one she is and the one she is becoming.

At home she has a tribal mask from Guinea of Ezili, the jealous goddess of love who never closes her crimson mouth. Dried chicken blood smears her forehead and sometimes Carnelia believes Ezili's wrath is her own. Also she dreams of the medusa mask, her boiling eyes turning men to stone.

Pictures of Carnelia' sister Opal flood her mind. Her masks, cancerous blue over bone throat, her eyes of smoke, wrangled hair. Rhapsodic eyes that crest and shatter like mirrors. Her wheezing breaths thick against the walls, like piles of shoes the Nazis stacked in numbered chambers. The masks of dead children, swollen angels, battered, sunken, Carnelia puts on all of these masks until they won't move, until they evolve into the rending of her form, her clubbed intelligence, the clotted burning of her song.

Bird-watching Carnelia and Ari Find the Avondale Swan in a Small Cove Outside of Watch Hill, R.I.

She is angora winged, glissading on water. She dips her neck, poising her tail feathers as she feeds on dark algae in the pull of the salt marsh. When she lifts her head she preens herself—a Queen before the mirror, forgetting the knavery of the King. She is all desire and white ashes strewn over the decks of burials at sea. She knows the secrets of dead mothers, what the murder victim whistles before the assassin rolls her into a white sheet. She is an ancient merchant, bartering feathers for salt. Where the sea rose withers, she lounges, lilts under eel grass. Imperial, she turns her back to the burning sun, folds herself into the shape of a bruised lily. She naps and dreams, moon lace over black water. When the moon swells she wakes and cruises under its glowing belly. Then she drops her eggs, like Baroque notes from a harp. The other one who has touched them with his burning, fans her. Shadows of white bouquets hovering by the embankment. Our Lady of the Swan.

Power Walking Sundown

No one taught Carnelia this: violet slats of light, collapsing between the tenements, breaking open mauve clouds, the wind dervishing dead leaves down Douglas Ave. Moving in front of Carnelia is the leather face of a chain smoker, eyes of a burned doll, walking to the store for another pack of cigarettes. All the plants are dead now in the window of Grayce's Unisex Salon. Kids poke at a dead squirrel cradled in the blow out of a truck tire. Their cries curdle the anorexic trees, while chimes swirl from the highest porch of a triple decker. When she passes, their cymbals ignite the light that blasts its angel trumpets up the oak tree. Three men drive by in a truck draped with pompoms. They make cougar noises at her, and she trips on a couch cushion flung into the dead leaves. The truck roars off and the blistered houses with their small windows surround her. No one knows she's there. No one taught Carnelia that the streaming of her blood on the last cliff of sundown could be this bitter sweet. No one but herself.

Salt for Salt

Though the sea is hollow, when you knock, she knocks back. Rock and she back rocks you. Swallow her and she backs swallows you. Down and down you coil in her until you fly, bursting for air, stinging the roe that sprung you. Salt for salt, you cut through her foam and she cuts through yours. She's made a swimmer out of you and you've made a goddess out of her and clung to her sparkling cleavage. She shares her diamonds willingly, so no need to wait until the will is read. "Mother," you call. "Mother," she answers. That night you both give birth to dark stars that rise over the kelp beds, over the black sea weed that is your hair. Inside the amnesia of dreams, her gigantic yawns launch you. There is a song about murder, bodies that never leave her.

Waking, Carnelia hears herself say, "This is your idea of a vacation?"

Chow Mein's Bone Box

Chow Mein whimpers. Someone has closed his bone box that's decorated with black roosters. He feels cheated, can't even nudge it open. He doesn't try to chew it with his daggery canines. No, this boy whines because the cruelty is too much for him. Carnelia assures him it's a mistake and that he can have his collection of steer hide-rawhide-calcium-dipped stumps. Gnawing is one of his finest talents. When Carnelia opens the box Chow Mein jumps up on her hip to let her know he won't forget her generosity. Something tells her these roles were once reversed. How else does she know his barking speaks for her? And when he sleeps, flinging his paws up to the ceiling, his legs splayed open, how does she understand his total abandon, the kind she only knows now during sex or sleep? Once she was the bitch, he the master, filling her bone box with llama bones. Her teeth recall long ago working over the rib of the white tiger.

Fortune Cookie: *"We Live on the Edge of a Miracle."*

Carnelia is not ready for spring. The forsythia bursts yellow as summer corn, but it's too cold. She begs Chow Mein to pee quickly, but he doesn't because the black M&Ms of rabbit turds lure him on. She shudders and the arthritis in her left hip aches in the dampness. But now she looks up to the fence post where a nut hatch balances, holding a white feather in its beak. This bird is not on LSD. It has the drive to gather, to use soft wisps to line the nest. Carnelia opens up her chest and spreads her feet apart. She stretches as far up and down as she can, and spits winter out. It's a bad taste like turned wine. Chow Mein chews on a dandelion, his yellow goatee. Let's break out the brushes and an easel for him. Carnelia will choose a buttery chardonnay.

Sassafras

for Robert Francis 1901–1987

Carnelia remembers the old poet who brewed her sassafras tea and made his own dandelion wine. He said she was a witch with words. Thinking of him in Fort Juniper with Gladys the hen squawking across the floor makes her laugh and cry. Robert, you never told me that one day I'd wake up, my body turning to stone, dried sassafras, like yours. I'm still spelling and misspelling with your seashell from New Brunswick—my paper weight—your breath turning in the lilac air.

High Flying

These are the high flying days of August. Carnelia watches clouds hoist their sails and fan out billowing. A flaming gourd, which is the sun, holds her in its orange meat. Her eyes shrink to slits. Her bones soak in the molten rays. They massage her sore knees and rotator cuff. At night the breeze swaddles her, cool. Her grief is a painting on someone else's wall. She finds dahlias the next day swaying in her garden, jugglers balancing multi-colored dinner plates on sticks that vibrate like toys. She tells herself, *If it rains tomorrow, don't forget this. Keep it, like a talisman under your eyes. It will save you from the gray drain of dying light that shrivels you and drags you down in winter. Don't give it up. Ever, this sway. Summer.*